The Adjustments

Claire Dyer holds a BA in English & History from the University of Birmingham, an MA in Victorian Literature & Culture from the University of Reading, and an MA in Creative Writing from Royal Holloway, University of London. She is the author of five novels and lives in Reading, Berkshire. *The Adjustments* is her fourth collection.

The Adjustments

Claire Dyer

TWO
RIVERS
PRESS

Also by Claire Dyer

Eleven Rooms (2013)
Interference Effects (2016)
Yield (2021)

Also by Two Rivers Poets

First published in the UK in 2024 by Two Rivers Press
7 Denmark Road, Reading RG1 5PA.
www.tworiverspress.com

ISBN 978-1-915048-16-5

1 2 3 4 5 6 7 8 9

Two Rivers Press is represented in the UK by Inpress Ltd and distributed
by BookSource.

Cover image: Pastel portrait study by Christopher Alexander, ARE, ARCA (1926–1982
used with the kind permission of his family.

Cover design by Sally Castle and Nadja Guggi
Text design by Nadja Guggi and typeset in Janson and Parisine

Printed and bound in Great Britain by Severn, Gloucester

Acknowledgements

My grateful thanks to the editors, competition organisers and judges
in whose publications, or lists of prizewinners, poems from this collection,
or versions of them, have featured: *Axon* C.4: Writing from the UK;
Finished Creatures 5 & 7; I Am Writing Poetry Competition 2023; *Mslexia* 2021
Poetry Competition; *Reading Stanza Shot*; *RiversSide*, Two Rivers Press;
Society of Women Writers & Journalists Competition 2018; *SWWJ* Elizabeth
Longford Poetry Competitions 2022 & 2023; *South* 57, 62, 64; *The Canvas
Arts Magazine* 1, 2022; *The High Window*, Spring 2020, Spring 2023;
Structo, 2015; *TYPE!* 1; *York Open Poetry Competition,* 2012.

Thanks are also due to Reading Stanza, Finding the Words, Martin Malone,
Hilary Hares, Sharon Black, Jane Clarke, The Lamb and the Retreats for
You poets, my Fresh Eyes clients for their inspiration and support, and
Two Rivers Press.

For Bea, Maddie
& any other Grands and Greats to come

Contents

The Last Of Them Takes All Night To Arrive

Around six next morning the low-slung exhaust
of his '97 Mustang scrapes the kerb as he pulls into the drive,
parks, puts his feet up on the dash and sleeps.
The neighbors stare as they leave for work,
as she watches from the stoop,
waits for him to wake.
There is a rodeo of birdsong and
his engine ticks as it cools.

He gets out at ten and she lets him in – jeans, check shirt,
cowboy boots. In the hall he tips his cowboy hat, says,
Howdy, ma'am. She gives him coffee, a plate of grits
and beans and, later, when he leaves, he kisses
her with his cowboy mouth, his lips soft
like velvet, eyes shining like the sun.

Perfect

Birdsong, and we unwrap the morning
like candy: pink sky, silver foil contrails.

We drink coffee, eat toast with warm butter,
thick cut marmalade, and talk

of the children – all their complications
and the wonder of them. We walk

next to a river and brush our hands
through the tall summer grasses, watch

the river birds – river water on them
like pearls, like sun.

Back home I make soup from the heels
of vegetables, you read in the garden,

in a low chair, canvas hat shading
your eyes; I hear you chatting to the cat,

then taking a call. The clock in the hall
strikes once, and we eat again,

making plans for next year, the one after.
Thank you, you say as I clear the plates.

The afternoon ticks by. You varnish
the house sign, I read in the garden,

in a low chair, the tide of shadows
washes the lawn, the birds

begin again and we have supper,
wrap the day back up: pink sky,

silver foil contrails. It is
as simple as and as perfect as this.

on arriving

what do you think the angel will say / and I'll look down at the cloud carpet under my feet / at its glints and whisperings / above us the blue will be sharp and infinite / *it's ok* I'll tell him / *it didn't take me as long to get here as I thought* / *will you stay* he'll ask / I'll reply *I shall try* / *the swallows are late leaving this year* he'll add / stretching his glorious wings so they'll make a sound like water falling / his smile will be luminous / and I'll say *how wonderful your certainty must be* / *how I wish I had known what being here means* / *before I made the journey to*

in the matter of silence II

there is the silence after the word grief

and the word breathes the air that is its sil

is the silence after the word dying

the air in the silence that is its oxygen

the silence after the word always

it begins and ends with it

silence after the word gone

it inhabits the space where to think

after the word loss

is the unthinkable and unsayable

in the matter of silence I

there is the silence after the word

is the silence after the loss

the silence after the gone

after the always

the dying

in the unthinkable and unsayable

it inhabits the space where to think

it begins and ends with it

the silence that is its oxygen

and the word breathes the silence of

and the silence breathes grief

The Woman Who Becomes A Field III

That, now she is warm and wise, the woman
asks questions of the sky, traces the crows' flight,
reads the words scritched on the white,
the blue, sees herself in the eyes
of minnows and water voles.
That she is a field and a stranger now,
she has to decide to stay or go. That,
she does this by lying in the lush grass
and the dry grass, by listening to the drumbeat
heart of horse, soil and stone, by holding
the rain in her palms, by breathing in
the frightening oxygen, by allowing
the astonishing dreams to come.

Montgomery, Fall 1940

Dearest,

Now that Autumn is soft and forgiving, the scent of molasses lingers and thoughts are of blown roses, I am thinking my love about our letters and our life in them.

We write to the moment, don't we – about financials and family, the friends who've been alongside, roadside on this 'Cruise of the Rolling Junk' (you see, I remember, and my love is for always and for your steadfastness)?

But should an English girl, or a Californian one, read this, in a book perhaps, with our pictures on the front, how will she know we were forever looking forward as well as back?

How can she ever know, my always love?

Devotedly,

Zelda

At Belle Tout

This summer. This summer of
hairdryer heat and parched
grass and us at Belle Tout looking
down at the cliffs, at the walkers,
their dogs, the sun spreading
its setting in flares and us holding on
to the railings, to each other, us
learning the ratio of saving
a life is twelve to one:
three chaplains, four coastguards,
two paramedics, the rest police;
the one sitting on the chalk edge
of Beachy Head, hood up,
completely still, facing out to sea.

At Bezirgan

The taxi driver stops
by the grain storehouses
at Bezirgan. It takes time

for the dust to settle
on the brittle grasses.
A vast sky bends

over us, sewn with birdsong
and heat. He tells us
these structures are a lost art,

stays in the car to check his phone
as we walk, speak in whispers,
touch the quiet, the warmth

of the wood. Our son
pulls away – his skin
gold and in the distance.

There is peace here,
space enough for this goodbye.
I feel it rise, the grief a thermal,

a shimmer against the blue.
Later, I'll say I love you,
you'll say you know I do.

The way back, in the village,
the driver inches around a dog
asleep in the middle of the road.

In Which A Fish Is Not A Fish

In the water it is beautiful,
can swim with the tide,

and against it, be invisible,
covert, then *shock*, it's visible –

see its scales rainbowing,
its fin-flick, its dark, dark eyes;

see it in the shallows,
how its body shines with the sun on it;

see its strength, length – don't
think about the stories of

the mating and spawning, the
incalculable distances it swims,

it in a net, and gasping. No,
remember it for itself, and its colours,

and you, leaning over the edge
of the boat, bridge, riverbank,

quay, cupping it in your bare hands,
holding steady for a while.

From This Before

Here is the black and white
garden of before, and I'm holding
what I know to be the blue
plastic bowl from before, and
it has Mum's vanilla ice cream in,
in the before, and she says, *Take
and keep the happy from this before*,
and I carry the bowl into the now
that will become the before, and
the bowl is full of the empty
before, and I remember her dress
with the roses on, and the sun,
like before, and ask, *How can this be
then, so long, so long in the before?*

In This Present

There is just one moon in this present
though somewhere will be water,

in its black fist a bright disc's movement,
and in its sway I am still your daughter,

though I am older than you now.
This minute's sky is a darkling blue,

and the stars we think we see in it will bow
their burnished heads, link arms and say they knew

this very moment was always to be ours
to keep, like film reel when it stutters

and the picture freezes. Hours
will pass and nothing matters.

You once made me a gift of wild flowers,
I'll live out my life with them 'til this moon shatters.

Nothing But A Cliché

This strangest of winters,
the clematis outside my window

is in bloom, and yesterday
I took five Marks & Spencer roses

for your headstone, one for each
decade you've been amongst

the acers and still water.
Just before the turning

to your garden, a deer,
stepping through the leaf mulch

on her reckless hooves, stopped
and watched me a moment

before disappearing into the trees.
Of course I believed

she was you dancing free –
a reminder, if I needed one.

Non Sequitur

Still winter and three daisies have appeared
like unexpected guests on the lawn.

We had paper decorations at *Levendale* –
a ball and bell stored flat but

when unfolded bloomed
with concertina magic. Year

on year we'd mend them with Sellotape,
hang them from the ceiling

in the hall as Nan made giblet stock,
the smell in all the softest

corners of my mouth.
Dad lifted me high then,

so I could tie the string and,
afterwards – a girl at hip-height

again – I'd watch Nan lay a doily
on her Victoria Sponge,

cover it with icing sugar,
lift the doily off, say, *Ta Dah!*

That was when I still believed
in snowflakes, love and fairy tales,

but will never tell you this, because
you are somewhere I can't be,

drinking tequila shots in a bar
with someone who's not me. The

daisies are trembling, or maybe sending
up flares. They should not be here.

Flare

The matchstick woman's been
the hiss and flare of sulphur

and its afterburn. It takes three
grown men – her son,

his two sons – to help her
down the beach club steps,

tuck the float around her,
push her off into the deep.

The sea is mirror,
movement, mirror.

She wears blue support socks,
white all-in-one that

would fit a child. She's
ninety-one years old, but

in the water is a girl
striking out for the deck

where he is always waiting.
She smiles, her bones are soft,

are softening, her sun-kissed
skin smoothing to a shine. She

tells herself its been worth the wait
to get back here to this first time.

'Our mother's house is built

from fish bones and silver plate.
In the windows of,

the flares are sun and sudden, and
she keeps countless

strongboxes in the attic of,
each the size of consolation.

In them are her sea storms,
and the ice, tempests that hurl

the trees, the leaves of,
at our feet. Here,'

the storm catcher's children say,
'our mother sang herself to sleep,

her fingernails still growing,
her few remaining teeth.

Soon we will waken her – gentle,
sore, say how close she came.'

My Grandmother Plays Tennis In 1916

Her mother's roses are past their best,
too weary to hear the pock of ball on string,
Mrs Manvers' boy chopping wood.

Scotland, lochside, and August;
late afternoon, the midges already tangoing.
The garden has vague corners and squares of sudden light.

Today she's smoked her first cigarette,
is wearing her brother's trousers,
hair tucked tight behind her ears,

is fourteen, losing heavily but doesn't care
because Douglas is here, he's home
on what will be his last,

last leave and when he wins
she jumps the net to kiss him
because she can, because the sun's

poured its salmon-pink onto the hills,
because it's before the Natterer's bats arrive,
before the firs darken at suppertime.

Chosen People

when you find your people
they will understand

the weight of dark
the sleepless hours

the hitch in your throat
that says you are afraid

they'll pocket your wish
that it could be otherwise

that you could start again
do it differently this time

they'll keep this safe and
will not blame you

your people will say it's ok
it will be ok

it always was ok
it's your heart's furies

that are difficult
but that's how it's meant to be

it's what makes the turning turn
is the how and when

and why of it
they'll promise you will not fall

tomorrow will be a remembering
you can be beautiful and

you'll believe this
all this as you step

beneath the songs of wrens
into the fields of wheat

Reimagining *Wild Geese* II

in the family of people
who could not love
but always made brutal the
every time you tried to travel
they told you
but you did this to please them
and you rarely pleased them
now
you are weeping
because
your family of people is dying
and   it
there will never be enough
forgiveness   the fields
where
in the morning it will already be
was always going to be
too late for
the dead of them will leave no footprints
no agency no love and

Reimagining *Wild Geese* I

Whoever you are, no matter how lonely,
the world offers itself to your imagination,
calls to you like the wild geese, harsh and exciting –

over and over announcing your place
in the family of things, in the family of people
who could not love *the soft animal of your body,*

but always made brutal the *heading home again*
every time you tried to travel *the landscapes,*
over the prairies and the deep trees, the mountains

and the rivers. They told you,
You do not have to be good.
You do not have to walk on your knees.

But you did this to please them,
and you rarely pleased them.
Meanwhile the world goes on.

Meanwhile the sun and now
you are weeping *for a hundred miles*
through the desert repenting because

your family of people is dying
and *you only have to let* it *love what it loves,*
there will never be enough

forgiveness *moving across* the fields
where *the clear pebbles of the rain are.*
In the morning it will already be,

was always going to be
too late for *Tell me about despair,*
yours, and I will tell you mine.

The dead of them will leave no footprints,
no agency, no love and, *Meanwhile*
the wild geese, high in the clean blue air, are …

Being Cecilia II

Coming in after being out
she is assailed, yes, assailed
by so many things:
tables, lamps, mirrors, spoons
collapsed in drawers
with green baize linings,
photographs, carpets and oh, so many books,
each like a postcard
from a place once travelled to.
She waits in the hallway as these
and all her other things hum a riff
that builds, builds into an earworm
more than the sum of its parts,
that is everything.

Being Cecilia I

In the days before, in a cab, in kitten heels,
gold lamé shorts, fake fur coat
that reaches her knees,
she's on her way to *Boom* in Poland Street
because Marvin says *It's radical, babe,*
and he's already half in love with Shea,
who pours shots behind the bar.
Once there, she checks her coat and knows
she will be swallowed whole by the jumping lights,
the jumping crowds because oh, these are her people,
people; because tomorrow, as Marvin's kissing
Shea in a kitchen in Kilburn, she'll leave
for work dressed in her mac and flats,
take an umbrella in case it rains.

Legacy

Amongst the rest, Dad,
you left me
ten rolls of carpet,
four pillar drills,
eight watering cans,
an industrial lathe,
seven tea sets, innumerable spoons,
your Elstow Edition
of *The Pilgrim's Progress*,
a carriage clock,
bits of broken vacuum cleaners,
three cold frames, a garden roller
from the Nineteen-Twenties,
a wonder of grandparents,
war stories, heartbreak,
a workbench of chisels,
Allen keys, screws;
you left me
top tips about insurance, a house,
two dead mothers,
your lawn mowers,
one Georgian sideboard,
recipes for Parkin
and Kedgeree, Handel's
music, your work
at Brockham Park,
my life – not
just once, but then again,
when I was five weeks old
and almost dying.

The Dead Dad Club

This late September evening
I'm joining the Dead Dad Club.

It's taken the long, quiet time
you've been gone

for me to believe I qualify,
but tonight, stripes of rosé clouds

over the neighbours' roofs,
planes shimmering in this autumn

sun, I am stepping up
to the podium.

I'm told I'm here because
I watched you die. It was

a slipping away. It was hard won,
at a time and in a place you chose.

It was with those who love you
by your side. I heard the last breath,

lived the absolute, the nothing
that came next. I walked

behind as they carried you out.
I buried you.

And yet, until right now
I didn't think you simply could not be.

The medal is a weight on my chest
as I take my place in the audience.

Deadheading The Roses

My sister and I are deadheading
the roses we didn't think you'd live
to see. We talk about small things,
not our mothers' deaths, nor yours.
Instead, we discuss the colours
of the petals, and how they fall
when touched, the slowness
of this, the grace. We gather
the drifts of bruised pinks,
yellows, reds, carry them fondly
to the compost heap that seems
to be waiting for you yet
to join us in your garden,
look up at the sky.

Between

When they tell me you are going to die,
I step forward to the edge, the edge
of the cliff, cloud, kerb, the water, and
lift my foot so it hangs, hangs
in mid-air, air which is cold and stitched
with things that glint, tiny things
I do not know the name of. And
when you do not die, not like they say
you will, I find I am falling anyway,
falling off the cliff, cloud, kerb, the water,
falling into the photographs I have of you,
into the things that are love and not love,
find I am between falling and landing, know
when I hit the earth, the world will split in two.

My Father, The Seahorse

I slipped out of you,
a coil of hopefulness
into the blue water,
can still fathom
how it feels
to be seahorse daughter
if I choose to,
in the waves, and
all the drowning,
measure the depth
of what is lost,
the lack of love,
the slaps in the space
of, in the face of,
you gave her
permission for,
and now, now
you are skeleton
only, it is too late,
far far too late
and yet, yet,
I am diving
to the seabed,
swimming your bones
to the surface where
the sun is warming
the blue water.

The day I went swimming with Theresa May

the first chlorine-hit brought back
Saturdays, Dad, and Bletchley's
municipal pool. Now Dad's mostly gone
and things moved on, the day I went
swimming with Theresa May
there was piped music,
two men simmering in the hot tub,
steam room with blue lights inside,
and Theresa, wearing bathing cap,
goggles, black all-in-one. Beside her:
no cap, no goggles, leopard-print
swimsuit, toes painted Berry Red, I
was the floozy of us two. And when
I say I swam with her, it wasn't
with with, but alongside
in the next lane, nodding to her shyly
now and then at the turn.
I left first, stinging from the water,
muscles weary, and oh so sad
to see her car outside
the club's front door, its engine
gunning, even there, security
guards talking into their lapels.
And, driving home on the day
I went swimming with Theresa
May, I thought about the rest:
Churchill, of course,
us floating like starfish,
him smoking a cigar in khaki bathers
like Grandpa used to wear;
Melbourne – Rufus Sewell-esque –
saying wise things as we bobbed
together at the shallow end;
both Pitts, without their wigs;
but not Maggie, Disraeli,
Chamberlain, Mr Johnson and the rest –

I haven't swum with them as yet,
but when I do, the late Queen
will be there and, should I beat them
all in the *Open Freestyle* race,
she'll daintily applaud,
and Dad'll be proud at last –
this being what dreams
are sometimes made of.

More Than Glass

Today through the window-pane
I see a lark high up against

the grey cloud,
and hear his song.

You are dying between
the snowdrops and the daffodils,

will tell me later,
when you briefly wake,

you're still waiting to see
the parakeets that arrowed

high above me as I arrived
and locked the car.

Without me to tell him,
how does this lark today

that I hear through the window
know it is his hour?

And later, when I sit next to you,
I will breathe with you as if

to gift my lungs, my heart,
knowing you will not see

this year's roses.
Two pigeons in the oak

outside your window
are burnished by this low

sun and, later, I will watch
them bow to one another,

balance on the branches
like ballet dancers.

No sound of voice or flute is
like to the bird's song;

there is something in it distinct
and separate from all other notes.

'There is more
than glass,' I'll say, holding

tight your hand as years ago
you held mine,

as, later, the parakeets will
fly over us once more.

It is years since I went out amongst
them in the old fields, and saw

them in the green corn; they
must be dead, dear little things, by now.

In these days of this dying

there's such trying, trying
to make patterns from the unruly, the
unruly and the random. Nothing coheres.
And yet, and yet, there's the fury of Brecht's
headlong stream, how we could/should also see
the fury of the river bed, its holding on, its
holding in. And yet, and yet, there's
kintsugi's celebration of breakage, of repair –
its gold-holding on, gold-holding in; oh –
there's that word beauty again – beauty
in the burr wood's holding on, holding in
the feather grains, making horse chestnut
into porcelain; there's your hand, your heart –
the holding on, the holding in – how your going
will leave visible the loss, the leaving, on my skin.

My Father Conducts *The Hallelujah Chorus* As He Lies Dying

He's been at it for months.
Each day his arms lift and fall
to an imagined music as he sleeps,
accompanied by the concentrator's

in-breath, out-breath, wheeze
of air mattress on the hospital bed
they've put in his room at home.
He has thickeners in his drinks now;

can't stand; can't stay awake;
is sinking into the sheet; is
missing the seasons –
gunfire of acorns dropping,

crack of frost, silence of snow,
riot of birdsong, snowdrop, leaf-bud,
soft April rain, and still he waits,
we wait, for his Messiah to arrive.

My Father Thinks Of His Father As He Lies Dying

The sparrow on the feeder outside the window
sees us – daughter and father –

both slowly dying. Dad is nearer his end
than I am mine, but still I know

it could all go in a snap – coming here,
a car wreck on London Road,

man in neck brace, four fire crew
cutting passengers from the back –

but mine will be the lesser loss,
smaller than my father's as he wakes again,

says his father should be getting in from work
sometime soon, this father who lay dying

thirty years before – skin yellow, bones hollow.
How can that be? Dad asks, reaching

for my hand once more, the sparrow lifting
into this spring sky – skitter of feathers, promise of song.

Fourteen

You told me you knew it was over when
the streetlights came on. Fourteen,

a boarding school dorm, a prefect
arriving with the news. How must it have been:

the dark, your mother weeping,
Aunt Kath taking cover

as her husband laid out pens, paper,
in Churchill's Rooms, your father

sidestepping that West End bomb;
how there was so little to eat, such

fear of fire, and loss – so many disappearing
tomorrows? And then that summer,

later and after Japan, lighting the beacon
on the clifftop, the scent and spittle

of burning wood, smoke in your eyes.
You could, you said, see the flames for miles.

Capture

It went like this, she says, knowing she's not
supposed to write of them, but heck,
why not try just this once to capture one
like it's a shooting star, hummingbird, pipistrelle?
There was a man – a West End concierge –
who wouldn't let me in his hotel, she says,
then he would, but because I'd just watched Killing Eve
and Konstantin had fallen oh so crumpily to the ground –

hand clutched to his heart – so too did my concierge.
Dream-me called an ambulance, she went on, *but*
then – and this is what might shock – his face
fell off, landing just in front of his head, his mouth

still moving, saying, Help, help me, please. The carpet,
she remembers, was kind of paisley, kind of pink.

On Sunday

she says where are the girls and they are the girls in pink crimplene
in an April church watching her marry their dad

she says where are the girls and they are the girls kissing boys
on street corners running home before all of the dark

she says where are the girls and they are the girls carrying the sharp
and the anger in the pockets of their coats

she says where are the girls and they are the girls in white dresses
holding lilies gypsophila astonishments of love

she says where are the girls and they are the girls with milk
in their breasts and babies who spin them in the small of their palms

she says where are the girls and they are the girls whose children
are grown leaving behind the dust and the words

she says where are the girls and they are the girls who say
we are the girls here in your house at your table on Sunday

our names on the forms that say you married our dad
that we were the girls in an April church in pink crimplene

girls who need to decide
she says where are the girls

Our Mothers Play Chess In Heaven

One dark-haired, one fair, sitting either side of a table –
County-schooled, parents friends, same husband
in the end – both dead now, now fable.

One moves her Queen, the other when she's able,
both heads bent, cloud-haloed, as the pieces land –
one dark-haired, one fair, sitting either side of a table.

One says, *The girls were mine, it said so on the label.*
The other lifts her Knight with fingers made of sand.
In the end both now dead, are fable.

One takes the other's Bishop. *One born July, one April,*
they say together, each holding up a hand;
one dark, one fair, sitting either side of a table.

One doesn't know if the other's grateful.
Both know it wasn't what was planned –
in the end, both dead now, and fable.

One arrived too early, one late, both painful.
We, your girls, are still trying to understand –
one dark-haired, one fair, sitting either side of a table –
in the end all are dead, all fable.

The Music For Our Stepmother's Funeral

We don't know what to ask for
but can't sit in silence, can't
have nothing but the windows
looking out onto the weather, so
choose at random: my sister says
she wants *Nimrod*, *The Lord*
is My Shepherd – and Dad, wrapped
in whatever music he, his wives
may have shared under
high white moons when
there were enough tomorrows,
says he doesn't mind but likes flowers
painted so the water droplets
on the petals look like rain.

The Woman Who Becomes A Field II

Now she is a field, she can collect the rain
from the leaves of ground elder and
hedge garlic, cabochons of rain to store
in the pocket of her second-best coat; now
she can understand distances and horizons,
how clouds breathe and the flavour of them;
now she finds she can talk to the hawthorn
shieldbug, tell it stories from her past, count
the underfeathers of partridge and grouse,
mimic the corn bunting's call, and all because
now, the late sun's colours have made her
something other, someone else, have wrapped
her in the warmth of stones, the wisdom of horse.

Duet For Telephone And Rain

A telephone rings in the house with tall windows.
April is fizzing in the trees,

tomorrow there'll be rain and someone who doesn't know
about the war has planted

circuses of daffodils, has tilled the soil to carpet, to
earthworm string and glisten.

This is, they'll say, a good year for magnolias. And Stanley's
painting goblets of blooms

to drink time from: blowsy blooms that bruise when touched.
Part flowering, part decay,

they move through the days intent on their awful blossoming.
Stanley picks up

his brush again; picks up his brush, begins again and,
off canvas, time has its hands

on the Baggetts' dining table, its nails pale, neatly trimmed;
restless fingers move a knife,

skin puckered around the joints, as Mrs Baggett knits,
stops mid-stitch, her husband speaks

into the telephone. A bus is carrying people home
in the rain. She knows our bones

are peeling back to marrow and it's always change
we're wishing for – one plain, one purl.

Drought

After the dry, rain deluges the dawn;
I hear our brittle lawn ease into it
and the eucalyptus, clematis, the Virginia
creeper on the back wall of the house.

Later, in the garden, by the Judas tree,
I think of ways to describe the scent
of earth: roasted sweet chestnuts perhaps;
midge-thick summer riverbanks

at dusk; that August evening,
dust on the piebald's back
as I led him to the lower field,
his tail swishing flies,

the day's heat in the tenderness of his hooves.
We are no good at drought you and I,
nor are our roses. I lift my hands
to catch the air, catch that false silence after rain.

The paving stones are damp, my feet bare,
the trace of rain under my nails, and I think
of you and me and the flood, how
to survive the dry, should it come again.

We leave Santos at once;

we are driving to the interior –
you, after surgery,

in the back seat of the car.
I corner carefully,

slow slowly.
We stop at a garage

for Mars Bars and tea
in Styrofoam cups,

then you sleep. Thin,
black trees, a sky

the colour of apricots,
the radio is playing:

Debussy, Chopin, a Volvo
advert, the news.

Arriving home, you wake
and we shuffle

to the front door.
Upstairs, I help you undress,

tender around your wounds.
In bed, you close your eyes

to this new landscape –
a destination

and a starting point
I never thought we'd reach.

Not only but also

at three a.m. with the night heavy
and freight trains on their insomniac tracks
to the city, to the docks, and the birds
not yet awake. I'm standing

at the window where here, on the other
side of the glass, our children could be calling
Look as dolphins swim their running stitch
through the worried water of the bay,

calling *Look* and pointing
with their spotless hands to the boats,
at the frayed green, yellow, blue paint
of the gunwales, and there will be

sea birds of course – oystercatcher,
cormorant, gannet, and the tap tap
of halyards against masts, and that taste
of salt and seaweed at the back of my throat,

and our children could be calling *Look*
as a sun rises huge and glorious, today
of all days, as the train's churn fades and
I get back into bed, still sleepless next to you.

The Surgeon Wife

Last night. The cat asleep at your feet.
I lift the covers and cut
the soft flesh of your abdomen. Each

move is fragile, silent, there's no blood
because of the magic, the early hour,
the clean moon. I see each rogue cell

glinting in the clean moon's light,
tiny as a star and as vast.
I tweezer them,

drop them into a silver bowl, the size
and shape of this love, this love, this.
I put back your muscles, capillaries, skin.

There is no scar, scar. I carry
the gleanings into the garden,
into the cold white light and

scatter them under the acer where
they shimmer awhile, then fade.
You do not notice that I've gone, are

still sleeping, and so is the cat,
his fur black and thick and wondrous,
his breathing matching yours, yours, yours.

Of Dark And Light

When I think of you
I think of you sleeping,

the dark pressing
down and, in the dark

I see your dreams,
the small escapes

of air from your mouth
rising to the ceiling,

circling the lampshade,
fading like they were

never there. I don't
think of you walking,

or city street, taxi cab,
gutters, the five o'clock

herds outside pubs,
cradling glasses, stamping

on cigarette stubs,
the look-at-me,

the no-care of it all.
No, nor you driving,

fingers tapping a tune
on the dash,

your shirt, your suit,
the way you rest

an arm on the window
ledge, indicate

when changing lanes.
Nor you, key in hand

on the doorstep of
the house, wearing

the weight of your day
as a scarf. No,

when I think of you
I think of you sleeping,

waiting with me
for the drop of the light.

Four Ways Of Looking At Dark

In the lane coming home from the kissing: she says, *In by dark*, but her inside with the lamps on and the sky already charcoal, and me outside in the not-quite-night, some stripe somewhere above the sea where the sun is still, I never know which version to believe.

Under the blankets is our country: we own it like territory; it has currency, flag and borders, seabirds, sunflowers and clapboard houses with picket fences, gravel on the drives; the fields smell of strawberries and your skin. In its weather is what we want to say if we knew the language and the words.

We watch the lights go out around the bay: think of an orchestra, the conductor on stage, saltwater in his shoes, baton aimed at the villas and the gardens – there is a kind of music in the certainty of this. The harbour is the last to go. We hear it roar as it falls.

Now all the yellow is in ribbons from the oncoming and the streetlights: the car is cocoon and lilac and you are arguing about the route – it's hard to see the road. Fists of condensation on the windows and the radio is humming to itself. The cats' eyes are our keepers.

Seduction

I'd bring it back if I could:
the gin-clear air, the spices, wine,

the music of it all. I'd bring
my skin tightened by the sun,

the million mirrors in the sea.
I'd bring market bustle, melons,

figs, and children shouting as they run,
kicking up dust, their eyes dark,

packed with words they don't yet know
the meaning of. I'd bring scooter hum,

men's hands raised in greeting
as they smile, say, *Merhaba*.

I'd bring the dip and dart of swifts
catching insects on the wing,

the sky lilac, swollen with the call to prayer.
I'd bring sparrow chatter

as dusk spills itself across the bay,
the moon a fingernail clipping in the sky.

Word Search: *yakamoz*

Across the bay the hooded moon
is undressing for the night,

it slips its cape into the sea; is naked,
voluptuous, saintly. Its white light

crowns each small black wave,
tasting as a tongue would.

The waves glitter as they come
cartwheeling into shore,

as the endless stars look down –
all this in just one word.

Raw Material

I carry the weather in my mouth.
Sometimes a damselfly
lands on my shoulder.
There is always so much sky.

Let me learn language enough to tell you
how a bougainvillea's shadow falls
like confetti on the terrace
when it's noon.

The cicadas rub themselves raw.
Are on repeat:
Stay. Go home.
Go home. Stay.

We are here
when the town's boats sail out
at sunset – a ring of boats
to honour the fallen.

We are here
when we cross the water to Kisla,
look back at the town's lights
sewn like diamonds into the hill.

We are here
and it's impossible to leave –
but when I do I'll carry this, and a disc
of sapphire sea somewhere near.

Any Old Iron

Materials for a bridge:
the lawnmower, some guttering,
a Boeing 737's wing,
all the saucepans we've ever owned,

and music, small beats and curls of it,
our children's first explorer cries,
off-cuts of carpet, the entire
Mediterranean Sea, that moonrise

over Kalkan, its quilted sky.
And, with rivets and the cold beer
we drank in *Sloppy Joes*, I fashion
a cantilever, throw across a line

of button thread, attach with steel pins
sheets dried in the wind
until it spans the space between us,
nothing beneath but salt

spray, gauze, the back-then Rag
& Bone man calling our mothers
from their kitchens, his horse
troubled by summer flies.

This relationship

is the	startling transformation of something tiny and fragile
	into something immense and indestructible
is	vaguely suggestive of a person
is	pure sex give*[s]* people permission to love
but *in*	it's really about you the intimacy of
	right here right now to know is an enrichment
you say but by *it's always*	blurring the distinctions just the way it was
	the holding together the awareness of breath

The moment the honeysuckle did its thing

I was at the end of the garden.
In the dusk, again.
The solar lights were on.
A blackbird was alarm-calling close by.
And the sky, this time, was like a mango.
And it was temporarily midsummer.
There was a small breeze.
It lifted up the scent.

The air was sweet and clear with it.
And it covered me.
And I got lost in it.
Temporarily.
And it was as unbelievably hard to let go
as it is to tell you this.

The Refusal

We finished the day
in the love seat

at the end of the garden
with the remnants of the wine

we'd had with dinner.
You asked if I remembered

it was in this spot we'd
decided to buy the house

decades before. *Yes*, I said, *I do*,
and, alone for weeks, that evening

we seemed peopled again
by our children and

the lives we used to lead,
and the dusk was lavender,

was sparrow
flit-and-dart, robin shouting

from the laurel, cat
rolling in dry earth as

the solar lights came on.
But none of this will be

this poem because it is
refusing to be anything

other than all the things
we couldn't say.

It was dark
when we went inside.

The last that spring

bloom like tiny sunbursts;
blaze as, day on day,

I draw the blinds against
the dark, the street,

the few remaining cars;
their fading imperceptible

until, touching one, I feel
nothing but the delicacy

of air, its valiant head bent
as if in mourning for what

we've never known we've had.
Afterwards, walking away

from the garden waste, their
shadows follow me and,

back inside, tiny specks
of yellow dust around the vase

like evidence of a crime.

Diving III

As we searched for it,
I watched you glean and gather,

slip in your knife, and twist.

Diving II

Eight feet down it grew cold, the ocean was
a weight of darkness, and breathing

hard until our gills came,
our skin splitting to let in the air.

I heard you gasp, felt the joy as you kicked,
dived deeper, deeper. Fish swam alongside

marble-eyed, with their swift fin-flick
and tails strong as steel. It took us years

to reach the seabed, its shipwrecks,
and the oyster shells.

Diving I

We set off young, and early, packed
for travel and for staying still, for mornings

and the inexplicable rains. The coast came
murmuring towards us; the boat we took

was yellow; restless clouds,
kittiwakes wing-dipping the waves

and when you said, *We're here*,
the sun was at its highest.

We were naked and un-knowing
as we began.

In Which You Marry Marilyn Monroe
Instead Of Me

You wake to thin summer rain,
your mother ironing, the church-

on-the-green breathing gardenias
and that slant-kind of silence

before the organ plays and, in a house
nearby, Marilyn is painting her nails

at the kitchen table, slipping into the hourglass
of a white satin dress – lips, kitten heels,

beauty spot – sashays through the hall,
practising her smile.

The car is waiting – a black Humber,
polished to a shine – sporting

silver ribbons, fake roses
on the parcel shelf, its engine running

and the rain stopping sudden for
the yellow summer sun, for the guests,

the flashguns, headlines
on tomorrow's news. You wonder

if she'll show as you wait at the altar,
your dad fit to burst – *That's my boy,*

that's my boy, he says – you thinking
of the beach, the subway breeze,

the promise in her voice,
her singing, singing voice, and

the congregation's rustling, light
splitting the coloured glass,

the organ sounding now Marilyn's
arriving, Rector John in his surplice –

handkerchief to brow – you
smiling your dazzling winner's smile.

In the city

the astronaut's lover's making
Banoffee pie, the post office
worker carries the taste
of stamp glue on his tongue,
a man's hand is on the shoulder
of a woman who will always
be married somewhere else,
in a bar downtown a waiter's
mixing a cocktail for a girl
in a red silk dress, it's below
zero and the pavements
smell of peaches and endings
when the story's worked out
the way it should, someone
with a sax on the corner
of Bedford and Main is
playing a song about the dark,
the moon's turning the pages
of *Madame Bovary* and the child
who was never born is watching
from a window counting up
to twenty and back to one again.

Limitless

I went to your funeral today.
There were hymns and prayers,

the choir sang Parry's *I Was Glad*,
the orchids on the altar winced.

Your wife sat at the front, and
someone called you *limitless*.

I watched your son's neck,
its soft nape, its impossible task.

And you stood at the vestry door,
the shape I knew of you,

and, afterwards, I slipped away
and you watched me go.

You bought me lilies at the station once,
and I asked you why.

You smiled and touched my hand,
Just because, you said.

This Stopped Moment

She says take it. In his hands it is a globe and warm.
In the park: leaf fall, the dogs are running,
a child in a yellow coat does not yet understand
there has been a summer, and high grasses,
and corncockles, ramsons, chicory.
Her hair moves like sea swell,
the colour of her eyes is peaty, no,
not peaty, but nearly. She will always

be married to someone else, says
fill your mouth with it. He lifts his hands,
puts it to his lips; it stops the din, the horse
mid-gallop, the open-throated bird.
She says I am this silence, find me in this forever,
I'll taste of longing and sweet figs.

Like Lovers

I meet you in a layby on the road to Llanberis.
        We get out of our cars.
The day's heat is syrup,

the lake water's smouldering.
        Our windscreens are flecked
with the carcasses of flies.

I remember you telling me once
        that a wasp's blood is pale –
the colour of straw – that eleven

percent of the world are left-handed.
        We'd been easy with one another then.
In the layby on the road to Llanberis

you raise your hand in greeting. Dust
        coats my syrup lips. I ask, *How are you,
how is she?* Your smile is like before.

Consent

As the film ended she said
he'd suggested text sex,

that she'd said maybe –
they'd discuss it next time

over roast pheasant at *Rules* –
that, last time they met,

the Meursault had buttered
her tongue, and when

he passed the salt
their fingers had touched.

The White Towel

so far in this not trust is
safer than the truth is

when she does her thinking
in the dark that's like wool on her face

and she's unpicking him again and he is
never who she thinks he is

is a turning turning thing
or maybe he is maybe he is

so far the towel is
white on the white sheet on the wide bed and is

what's left like limbs or love
when in her mouth is the taste of sex and soap

and leaning against the window is
the six o'clock train and the towel is

like the ones she's left before
that are white like white is

Almost Like A Murder

Pouring the wine he leans in,
his breath something complex.
He's wearing his blue shirt and
in the glass is firelight and earlier,
when he took off his coat.
She knows the wine will taste
of juniper and raspberry, watches
a drop travel down the bowl,
the stem, the base; watches as it settles,
like blood settles, on the table-top.

Later, and when it's done,
she stacks what's left, listens
to the dishwasher hum, and aches
to reach inside to touch the glass
they touched with both their mouths.
Her skin still is singing, and he's gone,
in his coat, his breath something
complex once again, and
she swabs the wine-blood-spot,
almost like a murder, from the table-top.

The Woman Who Becomes A Field I

That she becomes a field because she steps
from the roadside down to where the grasses
grow lushly even in high summer;
that she spreads herself thin under a paperwhite sky –
under the red kites' cries – spreads herself up and up
to the grazing of the field's solitary horse, and rests
her bones against his neck, his drumbeat heart;
that she reaches out a hand to gather
the day's heat from the dry stones of the wall
at the field's farthest edge; that the late sun breaks
the paperwhite sky into fragments of colours
that spill over her, the cornflowers
and buttercups, now she is a field.

Blame

He's the man of God explaining
the things of death, her imminent

grief, when she's six and they're holding
hands on a woodland walk.

He's the youth at Barry Island touching
her teenage breasts in the dodgem

queue and saying, *D'ya like that, doll?*
He's the boy she thinks she loves

who does not stop when asked,
whose student room she runs from,

whose neighbours give her hot
sweet tea, who's forgotten

it by morning. He's the barman pushing
her down on a foreign bed;

the work colleague saying
he likes her arse, another

wondering out loud
who she's had sex with to get the job.

He's the Sir in the Crypt of St Paul's
skimming her cleavage as he fingers

the badge of office on its red silk cord
around her neck. He's the six foot four

ex-marine on a train chatting
about his wife and kids,

then suggesting that she sleeps with him.
Why not? he says. *You look the type.*

The Half-Drawn Woman

His pencil is a hedgehog
tracking through the laurel.

You're seated, half-turned
towards the window.

Honeysuckle stirs against
the warm bricks of the garden wall.

You have never felt so known.
There, he says to you. *Stay there*.

You want to touch his mouth.
You want his mouth on yours.

You watch him watching, sketching –
pastels – pigments of skin –

hints of shadow, line. *There*,
he says. You're done. And

you're half-drawn, waiting
for the rest to come.

And even the sky

knows the hunger of the girl
in the supermarket queue, and
even the sky knows she'll choose
packets of air, tins of empty
and of whisperings to
feast upon, knows later
she'll dig out her throat,
sick up the air, the empty
and the whisperings, and even
the sky knows this will please
her, for even the sky knows it
will kneel, kiss the ground
before her, hungry for her hunger,
her pilgrim love of thin.

Appetite

Once I loved a man who ate bicycles.
Wintertime he'd kiss me with his metal-tasting mouth,
then travel to the frozen lakes to fish
ice holes for herring-flavoured spokes.

We'd have sex when he came back
and I'd find inner tubes in the bed.
In summer he'd travel to Maine to bake
bicycle pies and write me to say

they tasted of blueberries, cranberries,
pure maple syrup. In September
he'd cycle to Fethiye for tomato-pedals,
crossbars and tyres, bring bougainvillea blooms

home in his saddle-bag. We
never mentioned punctures, rain or rust,
but sped the country lanes with our backwards-
flying hair. *I love you too*, he used to say.

He left because I could not ride
the smooth cool water like he did, nor
smell the garlic in mudguards and gears,
freewheel through the snow.

The girl in Zizzi's ordering Penne della Casa

and drinking dry white
is me.

I'll have the same, I say
to a waiter with mink-brown eyes.

The sun beats
its palms against the window.

The glassware on the table
splits the light.

The girl looks at me;
I lean across and whisper,

You can't change what happens.
She breathes a curl of seabirds,

counts the tines of her fork, asks
So what is it I come to know?

Oh, how to word it –
each tulip,

bare feet on a woodblock floor,
first love, second love, third,

the children,
her wedding day,

how when gulls rise up from wet sand,
each wing-beat's a lifetime

and as brief.

Angel Delight

See the girl at the end of the hopscotch drive –
head at a cautious angle – waiting
for Clive Washbourne and
his Raleigh Chopper to arrive. Then, here it is!
Here he is: blaze of yellow tank top,
yellow bike. He stops briefly:
dark curls, dark eyes, smudge of freckles
across his nose, but she cannot speak,
so turns, turns in the incredible quiet
of that quiet afternoon where he remains,
is there still, in the silence of these impossible days
of hopscotch drives, pear blossom, grief;
her childhood surging back in birdsong,
in butterscotch on her tongue.

Instead

of waking in my grandmother's house with her in her yellow
dress, a Ford Cortina on the drive, Butterscotch Angel Delight
for dessert and my feet closer to my heart, I'm in a Hopper
painting again, telling you the Amish leave the flaws in the
wood they use for the furniture they make because this brings
them nearer to God, and that this is similar to us perhaps and
the still-life of damaged things in the service yard behind our
shop, and that oh, the church bells are sounding like teeth and
no one's using the doors the way doors want to be used because
it's Sunday and there's no washing on the line and I'm raising the
blind with the hyacinths on to look out at the street again, and
the old boy with the limp from the war, or so he says, is walking
his inconsequential dog, and in my head's the soundtrack from
High Society and Grace Kelly's moving beautiful like water across
the screen, all this.

Still The Girl

Brilliant sand, sun hot and huge,
the perfect day.

Us, the lane and valley sepia,
elderflower crazy, cliffs

sudden, sheer, and you
calling by my bright,

white house, us riding through
the haze, my bag across your back

and what was left of salt
and kissing sticking to our skin,

all the young of us picnic-packed;
heart pump and pedal pump,

the beach ours to echo and to roar in.
We hadn't learned to read the tides

but lay our limbs in the long grass and
knew we knew the knowing.

And, I'm still the girl, the thin-armed girl
who was your girl. Here's

the picture someone took for keeping
through the lifetimes and the leavings.

Hallmark

A story tremors:
a window, yard scattered

with dust and chaff, a white
stepping rooster – eyes

watchful as bullets – the sweet
scent of cattle; a girl

skimming the setting dishes
for the churn, hair damp

on her neck, breathing steady,
hand turning the barrel

pink from the sun. And when
it's done she'll print the yellow

with belonging: a piece
of sycamore – a tree, two birds,

their feathers the smallest veins –
will take bread, butter, meat, ale

to the field where he'll hold
a gold flower under her chin –

a hallmark the size of
a coin on her skin.

Soap

April sun much like this,
Mrs Hedges pinning

my child-body to the kitchen wall
with her one good eye as

she pauses in her merging of
two ketchup bottles,

the one we have already,
the other our new mother's

brought with her, with her pink
plastic hairbrush, her

ideas about soap, an antipathy
to cats and her husband's dead wife.

The cat and Mrs Hedges
leave us, but my sister and I

stay a lifetime, watch her,
our new mother, not Mrs Hedges that is,

save the remnants, the envelope-thin
slivers of Lux, or Pears, or

Budgens' own until she has enough,
wets them in the sink,

presses them with her gardener's
hands so she has a bar

as big as the bars you buy in shops.
It is, she tells us, a trick

from the war, and now
all our certainties have truly

disappeared, I do the same,
as I recall Mrs Hedges' one good eye,

the long-gone cat,
the brush's short, sharp sting.

The Frog Collectors

Playing out after tea – soil as dry as face powder,
leaves the colour of limes – we collected frogs

from the neighbourhood drains: yellow frogs,
green frogs, frogs the colour of tree bark,

frogs with seersucker skin, frogs with onyx eyes.
We carried them to the garage in our fishing nets,

built a frog paradise in the baby bath Mum took laundry
to the line in; gave them water, ferns for shelter,

Lego stepping stones, tempted them with morsels of worm,
tiny cuts of ham served in thimbles from the sewing drawer.

And, when I said goodnight, I touched a kiss
to each fragile, marbled head. We woke, of course,

to catastrophe, all frog promises broken; footprints
the size of fingernails already drying on the concrete floor.

Picture This

The worst winter for sixteen years,
Sylvia leaves her two children sleeping,
Dr Who airs for the first time,

seventy-thousand dissenters
march from Aldermaston to London,
Man U beat Leicester City 3-1 in the FA Cup;

JFK is shot twice – doesn't survive,
Clive Staples and Aldous pass away the same day,
the grassy knoll no Narnia, no *Brave New World*;

twelve-year-old John Kilbride disappears in Ashton-under-Lyne,
World in Action starts its thirty-five year run,
Harold Wilson (forty-six) takes his party's helm;

The Beatles have a trio of number ones,
£2.6m gets nicked in Ledburn,
James Bond is given his tenth licence to kill and,

in the garden of 13 Marlyns Drive, Margaret
wraps me, her second daughter, in a buttercup yellow shawl
for the photograph that sits in my bureau's fourth drawer

with the letters dated seven years later
saying how the countless people who knew her
are so sorry that she died.

When the tide comes in

is like that afternoon at Nan's with the doors to the garden
wide to marigolds and lawn, to croquet hoops and the water
butt, to the Surrey sky; like Nan's fancy cakes, sandwiches
on dainty plates; like Nan in her Sunday best pouring slops
into a special bowl – the saucers and cups tiny, thin as silk,
and as white; like me on not-an-uncle Uncle Bob's scratchy-
trousered knee; like him touching my small back with the
palm of his hot hand; is like you, Dad, when you later say
you don't trust that man at all.

What there was

was the length of your back curving
and the sun on it, and that sound,
that distant drawing of beast-breaths,

and the beast's neck,
its scales, sharp scissor eyes, and
all around us was sand,

wet rock, the dark and green of seaweed,
moon-pull, the slip-slip-slide of starfish
on the prowl. There we were Dad,

searching those sudden pools
of clear water for small crabs, sea anemones
that sway as though beautiful,

for limpets to get my nail under, touch
their soft underbellies and consider them
vulnerable. And, all the while, the taste of salt

was in my mouth and me
squatting next to you, Dad – treasure-finder,
dragon-slayer – me in shorts, plastic shoes,

sunburned skin. It was later,
with the sky washed,
the sea shining like sheet metal that

we took our haul home to show the others,
and still you didn't tell me
what happens when the tide comes in.

an idea of home II

for me it began with velvet curtains
the colour of spun gold   Campari   napkins
in silver rings   films
with enormous music   war and
horses brave as gods
it began afternoons after church   a
grandfather's voice
crowding the rafters   his garden   marigolds
in rows like soldiers and
the incessantness of traffic
began with a heaviness of secrets   rats
in a grandmother's cot   a child
buried at sea   the astringency of
asylums   madness   miniature roses
a yellow dress with poppies on   for me   it began

an idea of home I

it began   for me   a yellow dress with poppies on
asylums   madness   miniature roses
buried at sea   the astringency of
a grandmother's cot   a child
with a heaviness of secrets   rats
the incessantness of traffic
in rows like soldiers and
crowding the rafters   his garden   marigolds
a grandfather's voice
it began afternoons after church
horses brave as gods
with enormous music   war and
silver rings   films
the colour of spun gold   Campari   napkins
for me it began with velvet curtains

The Adjustments

The houses I've not lived in line the street I'm walking down in my fake fur coat and kitten heels.

It's trying hard to rain and there's a Mark I Escort parked up by the corner shop.

Outside are trays of earthy vegetables: King Edwards, turnip, swedes; piles of chillies, and kiwi fruit, priced in shillings and old pence.

I pass some childhood homes where my mother does not die, no stepmother with her perfect plastic brush arrives, and Dad is, Dad is, Dad is there.

Then I reach the racing green front door to number 4 where I move in with a boy called Paul who builds a perfect bookcase from packing crates. We have three children: Nancy, Clive and Ben.

Near the power station and football ground, I rent a flat with girls from work; we smoke weed on Friday nights, write poems in the early hours, sleep with each other, and a hundred men. Here, my heart remains perfectly intact.

Rye End, hedge fund Henry's Victorian villa is just before the park. Henry wears perfect shoes, smokes cigars, takes me hard, harder than I think he should. Here, our son starts boarding school at six, I leave at thirty-two.

By the dual carriageway is the Wyoming ranch – log cabin, fierce mountains, hot horse breath – where I live with Dex. Dex, whose lips are soft as velvet, eyes shining like the sun; Dex, who worships me perfectly, but can't give me any kids.

In the attic of the houses that were never built are the lost loves, the perfect loves I let slip away.

The rain comes when I reach this perfect cul-de-sac, move in with you, we have our son, our daughter-once-a-son; we sometimes laugh, others cry, plant our eucalyptus and our Judas tree, the adjustments of this life-real-life continue and begin.

Notes

'The Woman Who Becomes a Field III, II & I'
'The Woman Who Becomes a Field III, II & I' are after 'Gift' by Mark Roper

'Montgomery, Fall 1940'
'Montgomery, Fall 1940' is based on *The Love Letters of F. Scott and Zelda Fitzgerald*, eds Cathy W. Barks, Jackson R. Bryer

'At Bezirgan'
Bezirgan is a village in South West Turkey

'In This Present'
'In This Present' is after 'The Present' by Michael Donaghy

'Chosen People'
'Chosen People' is after 'Chosen Family' by Rachel Eliza Griffiths

'Reimagining *Wild Geese* I'
'Reimagining *Wild Geese* I' takes its italicised lines from 'Wild Geese' by Mary Oliver

'Legacy'
In 1958, Beecham scientists from Brockham Park, Surrey, found a way to obtain 6-APA from penicillin. 6-aminopenicillanic acid (6-APA) is the precursor of all semi-synthetic penicillins. My father was part of the Brockham Park team. When I was five weeks old I developed sepsis and Dad suggested I should be treated with a prototype version of this synthetic penicillin called Broxil; I recovered.

'The Dead Dad Club'
'The Dead Dad Club' is after *Grey's Anatomy*

'My Father, The Seahorse'
'My Father, The Seahorse' is after Jamie Cottle

'More Than Glass'
'More Than Glass' is after 'Snow' by Louis MacNeice and 'Field and Hedgerow' by Richard Jefferies

'In these days of this dying'
'In these days of this dying' was prompted by *Oh Beautiful World!* a sculpture in burr wood by Eleanor Lakelin for Reading Museum, 2021

'The Music For My Stepmother's Funeral'
'The Music For My Stepmother's Funeral' is after Faith Shearin

'Duet For Telephone And Rain'
'Duet For Telephone And Rain' is after *Magnolias, 1938* and *Portrait of Mr and Mrs Baggett 1956–7*, The Stanley Spencer Gallery

'We leave Santos at once;'
'*We leave Santos at once;*' is after 'Arrival at Santos' by Elizabeth Bishop, *Questions of Travel*, 1965

'Word Search: *yakamoz*'
yakamoz is the Turkish word for moonlight on water

'*This relationship*'
'*This relationship*' is a found poem, after Jeff Koons at The Ashmolean, 2019

'The Half-Drawn Woman'
'The Half-Drawn Woman' was inspired by a sketch by Christopher Alexander, Turner Contemporary, Margate, 2015 (see note on back cover)

'Hallmark'
'Hallmark' is based on a butter print from The Sharp Collection, Museum of English Rural Life, Reading

'an idea of home'
'an idea of home II & I' are after Penelope Shuttle

Two Rivers Press has been publishing in and about Reading
since 1994. Founded by the artist Peter Hay (1951–2003),
the press continues to delight readers, local and further afield,
with its varied list of individually designed,
thought-provoking books.